S0-AIP-985

Hayner Public Library District-Alton

0 00 30 0397866 9

HAYNER PUBLIC LIBRARY DISTRICT
ALTON, ILLINOIS

OVERDUES .10 PER DAY MAXIMUM FINE
COST OF BOOKS. LOST OR DAMAGED BOOKS
ADDITIONAL $5.00 SERVICE CHARGE.

MUSICAL INSTRUMENTS OF THE WORLD

Stringed Instruments

M. J. Knight

A+
Smart Apple Media

HAYNER PUBLIC LIBRARY DISTRICT
ALTON, ILLINOIS

Published by Smart Apple Media
2140 Howard Drive West, North Mankato, Minnesota 56003

Designed by Helen James

Photographs by Corbis (Art Underground, Cheque, Anna Clopet, GIANSANTI GIANNI/CORBIS SYGMA, MC PHERSON COLIN/CORBIS SYGMA, Pablo Corral V, Henry Diltz, Kevin Fleming, Michael Freeman, Rune Hellestad, Dave G. Houser, Robbie Jack, Kelly-Mooney Photography, Bob Krist, Barry Lewis, Chris Lisle, Gail Mooney, Gianni Dagli Orti, PACHA, Neal Preston, Bob Rowan; Progressive Image, Royalty-Free, Tom Stewart, Nik Wheeler, Adam Woolfitt, Conrad Zobel)

Copyright © 2006 Smart Apple Media. International copyrights reserved in all countries. No part of this book may be reproduced in any form without written permission from the publisher.

Printed in Thailand

Library of Congress Cataloging-in-Publication Data

Knight, M. J.
Stringed instruments / by M. J. Knight.
p. cm. — (Musical instruments of the world)
Includes index.
ISBN 1-58340-414-7
1. Stringed instruments—Juvenile literature. [1. Stringed instruments.] I. Title.
II. Musical instruments (North Mankato, Minn.)

ML750.K55 2004
787'.19—dc22   2003070352

First Edition

9 8 7 6 5 4 3 2 1

J787.19
KNI

617179208

Contents

Introducing Stringed Instruments

This book is about the musical instruments that belong to the string family.

Stringed instruments make a sound when their strings vibrate. The strings are bowed, plucked, or struck to make their sound. When they are played, the whole string vibrates from one end to the other.

The strings don't make much sound on their own. The vibrations they make pass to a thin soundboard

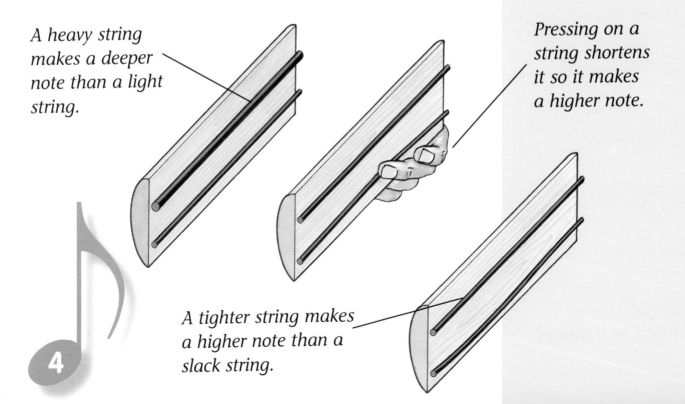

A heavy string makes a deeper note than a light string.

Pressing on a string shortens it so it makes a higher note.

A tighter string makes a higher note than a slack string.

4

underneath, which also vibrates, making the sound louder. Some stringed instruments also have hollow bodies, which resonate to make the sound louder still. The sound holes in the body of the instrument allow the sound to escape.

These violinists played a concert for Pope John Paul II when he visited Venezuela in 1996.

The strings have to be strong and are usually made of nylon or steel. A light string makes a higher note than a heavy string that is the same length. String players can also make higher notes by pressing a finger on a string to shorten it. The tighter the string is, the higher the note it makes.

Stringed Instruments

Violin

Violin Violin Violin

The beautiful curved shape of the violin was created in Italy about 500 years ago. The violin shares its shape with a whole family of stringed instruments: the viola, the cello, and the double bass. As the baby of the family, the violin is small enough to be tucked under the chin.

The hollow wooden body of the violin has four strings stretched over it. When the violinist pulls a bow over the strings, they vibrate and make a note. The hollow body makes the sound louder.

Violinists put a soft pad under their violin to make it more comfortable to play.

You can hear violins playing classical music in orchestras and string quartets. Another name for the violin is the fiddle. It is sometimes played in folk, rock, and jazz bands.

Violins are made by hand from slices of pine or maple wood. The violin maker glues together two pieces of wood to make the front and two to make the back. A fine saw is used to cut out the curved shape.

The sides of a violin are called the ribs. They are made from strips of wood molded into shape and glued between the back and front.

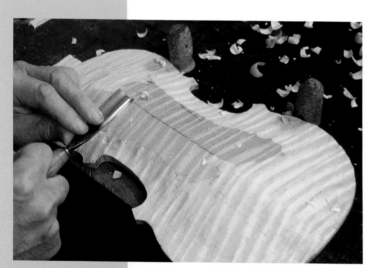

Two F-shaped sound holes are carefully cut out of the body. The carved neck and scroll are added.

TOP A sharp chisel is used to shape the back of the instrument.

BOTTOM Shaping the scroll of the violin.

Viola Viola Viola Viola

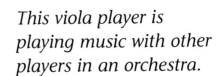

The viola is the violin's big sister. It is still small enough to fit under the player's chin, but the sound it makes is lower and richer than the sound of the violin.

The viola's four strings are played with a bow in the same way as a violin. Viola players also make notes by plucking the strings with the fingers of their left hand. This is called "playing pizzicato."

Most viola players belong to an orchestra or a string quartet. You do not often hear the viola played on its own as a solo instrument.

This viola player is playing music with other players in an orchestra.

Cello Cello ♪ Cello Cello ♪

The third-largest instrument in the violin family is the cello, also called the violoncello. The four thick strings of the cello play lower notes than the strings of a viola.

To play the cello, players have to sit down with the instrument leaning toward them, so the scroll is over one shoulder. A metal spike keeps the cello off the floor. Cellists use a short wooden bow or pluck the strings with the fingers of their left hand.

This cellist is playing the cello with a wooden bow.

Did You Know?

Hairs from horses' tails are used to make bows for the string family. Smooth, pale hairs work best. It takes 200 hairs to make a cello bow, 175 hairs for a viola bow, and 150 for a violin bow.

9

Double Bass

Double Bass
Double Bass

The double bass is the granddaddy of the violin family. It can be more than five feet (1.5 m) tall from the spike resting on the floor to the scroll at the top.

Double bass players have to stand up or sit on a high stool to play. When they pull a bow across the strings, the double bass makes a low, full sound. The strings of a double bass can be plucked, too, to make a deep, echoing sound.

In jazz or folk music, the double bass plays the rhythm. An orchestra usually has several double bass players.

This double bass is part of the American jazz band the Brian Setzer Orchestra.

The Violin Family in an Orchestra

The sound an orchestra makes comes from many different instruments. A symphony orchestra is divided into four sections: stringed instruments, woodwind, brass, and percussion. It has about 90 musicians and plays classical music.

The string section is an important part of an orchestra.

There are usually 30 violinists in an orchestra. The stringed instruments are arranged at the front, and the musicians who play louder instruments stand or sit behind them.

A conductor leads the orchestra. He or she uses hand movements or a small stick called a baton to show the musicians how fast and loud to play.

Harp Harp Harp

The very first harp was inspired by the shape of a hunter's bow more than 5,000 years ago. Today, harps of many different shapes and sizes are played all over the world.

The orchestral harp is a big, triangle-shaped instrument. It has 48 strings of different lengths stretched between the top and the side.

When harpists sit down to play, they tilt the harp onto one shoulder. They play the higher (shorter) strings with their

This Egyptian wall painting shows a harpist performing more than 3,000 years ago.

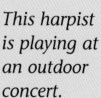

This harpist is playing at an outdoor concert.

right hand and the lower (longer) strings with their left.

Harpists can make a beautiful wave of sound called a glissando by brushing their fingers across the strings. The harp also has seven pedals that change the notes made by the string when they are pressed.

Did You Know?

The strings of orchestral harps are different colors to make it easier for the harpist to find the right one to play.

Harp Harp Harp

This lutenist is playing the lute in a theater production of a play by William Shakespeare.

Lutes are the oldest relatives of the violin and guitar. People have played lutes for more than 4,000 years.

A lute is shaped like half a pear. Its wide neck ends in a pegbox, which is bent backward at an angle to the neck.

Old lutes have as many as 20 strings. Covering the strings with four fingers is difficult, which is one reason that lutes are not often played today. Another reason is that lutes are very hard to tune, and lutenists (people who play lutes) may spend as much time tuning the instruments as they do playing them.

Did You Know?

The charango is a small lute from South America that is made from the horny skin of the armadillo, a small digging animal that comes out at night.

14

Balalaika Balalaika

Have you ever seen or heard a balalaika? This Russian instrument developed from the lute. Its wooden body is shaped like a triangle and has a flat back. Many people think of the balalaika as the national instrument of Russia.

Balalaikas come in six different sizes. From the smallest to the largest, they include: the piccolo, the primo, the secunda, the viola, the bass, and the contrabass. The contrabass plays very low notes. All balalaikas have just three strings.

Balalaikas play folk music and accompany energetic Russian folk dances.

This balalaika is almost as big as its player.

Mandolin
Mandolin Mandolin

The mandolin has a pear-shaped body, with a deep, rounded back. Many mandolins are beautifully decorated. They have four pairs of metal strings that the mandolin player plucks with a plectrum to make a "shimmering" sound.

Did You Know?
The mandolin is named after its shape. The Italian word *mandolino* means "little almond."

The mandolin comes from Italy, where mandolin players often play a tune (or melody) accompanied by a guitar. There are also several larger-sized mandolins, called the mandora, mandocello, and mandobass. They are all played together in a mandolin band.

Blues musicians often play the mandolin and other stringed instruments.

Bouzouki Bouzouki
Bouzouki Bouzouki

This bouzouki player is strumming a set of strings with a plectrum.

The bouzouki is a Greek folk instrument. It looks like a long-necked lute and has a rounded, wooden body.

Metal frets divide up the long neck of the bouzouki. Eight metal strings are arranged in twos, and each set plays the same note.

The bouzouki player plays a tune by strumming one set of strings with a plectrum.

Banjo Banjo Banjo

The first banjos were made hundreds of years ago in West Africa from gourds (small, pumpkin-like fruits). The gourd was cut in half, and a piece of sheepskin was tied tightly over the top.

Today, banjos have round, wooden bodies and steel strings: four long strings and a fifth, shorter string. Banjo players pick out the tune with their thumb on the short string and play the accompaniment on the other four strings with their fingers.

The banjo is most often played in folk bands.

Emily Robison plays banjo in the American country music band the Dixie Chicks.

Ukulele Ukulele Ukulele

Isn't "ukulele" a fun word to say? It means "jumping flea" in Polynesian. The ukulele is a small guitar that was first played in Hawaii. It developed from a fish-shaped Portuguese instrument called the machete.

Ukulele players pluck or strum the four nylon strings, making a light, twanging sound. Ukuleles became very popular in North America and Britain during the 1930s. Today, they are most often heard in folk bands.

These Hawaiian ukulele players produce a twanging sound by strumming the strings.

Did You Know?

A cross between the banjo and ukulele was invented in 1925. It was called the banjulele.

Sitar Sitar Sitar Sitar Sitar

The sitar is a famous Indian instrument. Its body was once made from a gourd, and it has a very long neck.

Sitars have six or seven main strings that are played with a plectrum. The highest-sounding string plays the tune. Up to 19 more strings are held by small pegs on the sitar's neck, and these make an echo sound when the main strings are played.

These schoolboys in India are learning to play the sitar.

Sitar Sitar Sitar Sitar Sitar

Sitar

Did You Know?

Classical Indian music follows tunes and rhythms called ragas and talas. Different ragas are played at particular times of the day: for example, a late-morning raga, or a night one. There are also special ragas for every season.

Every sitar has 20 metal frets across the neck. These frets can be moved to play different tunes. Sitar players change a note by pulling a string sideways across a fret and making the note slide or waver.

Sitar players sit cross-legged on the floor, with the instrument across their knees. The sitar usually plays solos, accompanied by the tabla and the tambura.

Sitars are too large to be held, so they are rested on the floor.

Zither Zither Zither

The ground zither was created hundreds of years ago, in Africa, when someone stretched a piece of string between two posts in the ground. A hole was dug under the string, and the string was hit with a piece of wood to create a rhythmic sound.

Today, zithers are played all over the world. Europeans play board zithers. These shallow, wooden boxes have one straight and one curved side, with 45 strings stretched over the top.

Zither players sit with the instrument on their lap or on a table in front of them. They play the tune with their right thumb on the five strings on the straight side of the zither. Their fingers play the accompaniment on the other strings. Their left hand holds down the strings to make the notes.

A traditional African ground zither string stretched between two twigs over a hole in the ground.

Dulcimer

The dulcimer is played by hitting the strings with small hammers. You can often hear it in the mountains of Austria and Switzerland.

These musicians are playing their dulcimers outdoors in Finland.

Cimbalom

The Hungarian cimbalom might be mistaken for a table, because it stands on four wooden legs. Players tap the strings with thin wooden beaters covered in soft cloth to create a warm, ringing sound.

This cimbalom is part of a gypsy band.

Koto Koto Koto Koto

The elegant Japanese koto has looked the same for hundreds of years. Its curved, wooden body is 6.5 feet (2 m) long and holds 13 strings. Long ago, the strings were made of silk, but today they are usually made of nylon.

Each string on a koto has its own bridge shaped like an upside-down Y. Bridges hold the strings away from the body so they sound more clearly. Bridges can also be moved to retune the string.

Koto players wear plectrums that look like small thimbles and fit over the thumb and first two fingers of their right hand. The koto is often played as a solo instrument, or to accompany other instruments or singers.

Did You Know?

When a group of instruments plays gagaku (Japanese classical music), the koto plays the tune. It is accompanied by pipes called shawms, lutes, and drums.

This musician kneels on the floor to play her koto.

The bandura is an unusual-looking instrument from the Ukraine, with a flat back and more than 40 strings. It looks like a cross between a zither and a lute, and it sounds like a small harp.

A group of Ukrainian bandura players at a concert.

Some banduras have two necks, or scrolls. The low, longer strings run up the neck, while the high, shorter strings are attached to the body of the instrument. Bandura players pluck the low strings with their left hand and play the tune on the high strings with their right.

The body of an acoustic guitar is shaped like the number eight. It developed in North Africa and was brought to Europe 400 years ago. Today, guitars play both popular and classical music all over the world.

Frets run across the fingerboard of an acoustic guitar. The instrument's six strings are made from nylon or steel. Guitarists place their fingers over the strings in different positions on the frets to make notes. Several notes played together create a chord.

This guitarist is plucking the strings with her right hand while she holds them down with her left hand.

Guitarists pluck the strings with their fingers or strum across them with a plectrum. Do you know someone who plays the guitar?

Dobro

Dobro Dobro Dobro

This acoustic guitar has a metal resonator disk inside the body. The disk was added to make the guitar's sound louder.

Guitarists often play the dobro with a bottleneck, which is a metal tube fitted over a finger and pressed against the strings. Some rock and blues musicians play the dobro. It can also be heard in some country songs.

The metal resonator sits in the body of the dobro and makes the guitar's sound louder.

Electric Guitar

Electric Guitar

The electric guitar plays rock and pop music. It has a solid wood or plastic body and six steel strings. The fingerboard has frets across it that show guitarists where to put their fingers.

Guitarists play with a plectrum. The vibrations made by the strings pass through a pickup under the strings. They are made louder by a machine called an amplifier that is connected to the guitar. The sound travels through the amplifier and out through speakers.

Did You Know?

A man named Leo Fender invented the first guitar with a solid body in 1944. His most famous and successful guitar is the Fender Stratocaster, which top guitarists still play.

This electric guitar is connected to the amplifier by a long cable.

28

Hawaiian Guitar

The Hawaiian guitar (or pedal-steel guitar) is an electric guitar that creates a swooping, sliding sound (a glissando). Guitarists move a steel bar up and down the strings to produce the sound.

Country-rock music is often played on pedal-steel guitars.

Electric Guitars in Bands

Most rock and pop bands have two or three electric guitars. One is the lead guitar, which plays solos. The second is the rhythm guitar, which plays rhythmic chords. The third is the bass guitar, which plays low notes beneath the other two guitars.

Members of the rock band Dire Straits performing with guitars on stage.

Like all electric guitars, the bass guitar is also made from solid wood or plastic, but it usually has only four thick, heavy strings. Its controls are similar to those of six-stringed guitars.

Words to Remember

accompany Play alongside a singer or another musician who is playing the tune.

amplifier A machine that makes sounds louder electronically.

blues Sad and rhythmic folk songs that originated in the southern United States more than 100 years ago.

bridge A small piece of wood that holds the strings away from the body of an instrument. The bridge allows the strings to sound clearly.

classical music Serious music is sometimes called classical music to separate it from popular music. Classical music can also mean music that was written during the late 18th and early 19th centuries and follows certain rules.

country Music that had its beginnings in North American cowboy songs. Also called country and western music.

fingerboard A strip of wood glued to the neck of a string instrument that players press to make different notes.

folk Traditional songs and tunes that are so old that no one remembers who wrote them.

frets Small metal bars across the fingerboard of some string instruments, such as the lute or guitar. Frets help players find the correct position for their fingers when sounding notes or chords.

jazz A type of music played by a group of instruments in which each one plays its own tune. Jazz musicians often improvise, or make up, the tunes they play.

plectrum A small piece of plastic used to pluck string instruments. It is also called a pick.

pop Popular music that is entertaining and easy to listen to.

resonate Resound or echo.

rock Pop music with a strong beat, or rhythm.

scroll The carved top of a stringed instrument, such as a violin.

string quartets Groups of four musicians playing two violins, a viola, and a cello.

tambura A long-necked instrument from India, often played with the sitar and tabla.

tune Adjust an instrument so that it makes the correct sounds. If an instruments isn't tuned, it will play notes that sound either too high or too low.

varnishes Paints on a clear coat of liquid resin, which is shiny when it dries.

vibrate Move up and down quickly, or quiver. A string vibrates when it is bowed, plucked, or hit.

Index